A New True Book

ASTRONAUTS

By Carol Greene

 CHILDRENS PRESS, CHICAGO

These seven men were America's first astronauts. They were selected in 1959 for the Mercury Program. Front row, left to right, are Walter M. Schirra, Jr., Donald K. Slayton, John H. Glenn, Jr., and M. Scott Carpenter. Back row, left to right, are Alan B. Shepard, Jr., Virgil I. Grissom, and T. Gordon Cooper, Jr.

PHOTO CREDITS

Historical Pictures Service, Chicago—4 (2 photos), 7, 8

Wide World Photos—10, 13, 15

NASA: National Aeronautical & Space Administration—12, (2 photos), 16, 17, 22 (2 photos), 24 (2 photos) 27, 28, 29, 30, 31, 32, 33, 34 (2 photos), 36 (2 photos), 37 (3 photos), 38 (2 photos), 41, 43, 45

Holiday Film Corporation—11, 19 (3 photos), 20

Library of Congress Cataloging in Publication Data

Greene, Carol.
  Astronauts.

  (A New true book)
  Includes index.
  1. Astronautics—Juvenile literature. 2. Astronauts—
Juvenile literature. I. Title.
TL793.G76 1984   629.4'023   83-23142
ISBN 0-516-01722-5   AACR2 144660

TABLE OF CONTENTS

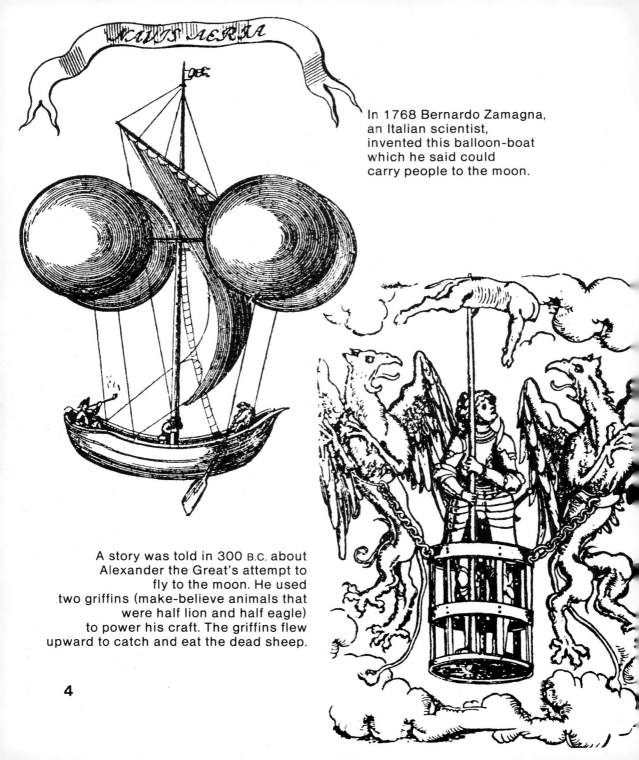

NAVIS AERIA

In 1768 Bernardo Zamagna, an Italian scientist, invented this balloon-boat which he said could carry people to the moon.

A story was told in 300 B.C. about Alexander the Great's attempt to fly to the moon. He used two griffins (make-believe animals that were half lion and half eagle) to power his craft. The griffins flew upward to catch and eat the dead sheep.

4

A DREAM COME TRUE

For many years people dreamed of traveling in space. What would it be like? What would they find? Could they fly all the way to heaven? Were there really little green people on Mars?

In 1777, Franz Joseph Haydn wrote an opera called *The World on the Moon*. In it some people visited the moon. The moon looked different. But the people sang and joked and wore beautiful clothes—just as if they were on earth.

Around 1780, a man in France invented a spaceship. It was a basket tied to a balloon. People rode in the basket.

Jules Verne
wrote about
a moon train in
*From the Earth
to the Moon.*

Jules Verne, a writer,
knew a lot about science.
In 1865, he wrote about a
"moon train." It looked like
a rocket with cars attached.

German astronomer,
Johannes Kepler

Meanwhile, scientists were studying space. In the 1600s, Johannes Kepler had figured out that planets moved around the sun in orbits. His ideas are used in space travel today.

In the 1900s, more and more scientists began working on rockets. Russians, Germans, and Americans all tried to find a way to get into space.

Then, on November 3, 1957, the Russians sent up the first space traveler. She was a dog called Laika. But the Russians had no way to get her back. She died in space.

So the dream did not
really come true until
April 12, 1961. On that
day, a Russian, Yuri Gagarin,
orbited the earth one time.
He was the first human
being to travel in space.
And he came back safely.

Major Yuri Gagarin
was the first man
in space.

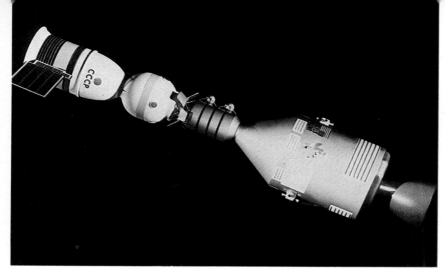

America's Apollo spacecraft (right) docked with the Russian Soyuz spacecraft in 1975.

FAMOUS FIRSTS

Russian space travelers are called cosmonauts. That means "universe sailors." American space travelers are called astronauts. That means "star sailors." Both words come from the Greek language.

11

Astronaut Alan B. Shepard, Jr. (left) and John H. Glenn, Jr. (right)

Alan Shepard was the
first American in space.
On May 5, 1961, he flew
for fifteen minutes. But he
did not orbit the earth.
John Glenn was the first

astronaut to do that. On
February 20, 1962, he
went around the earth
three times.

Then, in 1963, Russia sent
the first woman into space.
Valentina Tereshkova circled
the earth forty-five times.

Cosmonaut Valentina Tereshkova

After that, more and more astronauts and cosmonauts traveled in space. In 1964, the Russians sent up three cosmonauts in the same spacecraft. One was a pilot, one was a medical doctor, and one was a scientist.

On March 18, 1965, a cosmonaut, Alexei Leonov, took the first space walk. He had a wonderful time. He could look right down on the Soviet Union.

Lieutenant Colonel Alexei Leonov (left) and
Colonel Pavel Belyayev (right)

"I felt as though I were
floating over a huge
colored map," he said.

In 1965, the United
States began its Gemini
program. Two people could
travel in a Gemini
spacecraft. There were
twelve Gemini flights in all.

Astronaut Edward H. White II. In 1967 he died in a fire aboard the Apollo spacecraft with Astronauts Grissom and Chaffee.

The Gemini astronauts practiced hooking up their spacecraft with others. Edward White became the first American to walk in space. He had such a

The operations control room watches over all space flights. You can see pictures from space on the TV screen.

good time that he didn't want to come back in.

Spaceflights were getting longer and longer. In 1966, the United States began its Apollo program. In 1968, *Apollo 7* sent back live TV pictures and sound from space. That same year, *Apollo 8* orbited the moon ten times.

Then, on July 20, 1969, Neil Armstrong and Edwin Aldrin became the first men to walk on the moon.

Armstrong stepped on the moon first. The whole world watched on TV and listened as he climbed down the ladder. His foot touched the moon and he said, "That's one small step for a man, one giant leap for mankind."

Edwin Aldrin (above) was the second human to step on the moon. The Americans left a flag, a plaque, and their footprints behind. Aldrin (left) and Armstrong were kept away from people when they first returned to earth. This was to make sure they had not brought back any mysterious moon diseases.

Apollo 2 orbits the moon as the earth rises over the moon's horizon.

Almost a day later, Armstrong and Aldrin flew back to Michael Collins in the command module. But behind on the moon they left a plaque.

It said "Here men from
the planet earth first set foot
upon the moon, July, 1969 A.D.
We came in peace for
all mankind."

After that, there were
more moon landings.
Astronauts and cosmonauts
set up space stations.
They spent longer and
longer times in space.
They ran all sorts of
scientific experiments.

Astronauts Guion Bluford and Sally Ride.

Sally K. Ride became
the first American woman
in space on June 18, 1983.
She is an astrophysicist
and did important scientific
work on that flight.

When it was over, she said, "The thing I'll always remember about that trip is that it was fun."

In September of 1983, Guion Bluford became the first black American to travel in space. He helped with medical experiments.

One of these experiments was sent up by Dr. Paul E. Lacy. It may help Dr. Lacy find a cure for diabetes someday. And that would be another first for space travel.

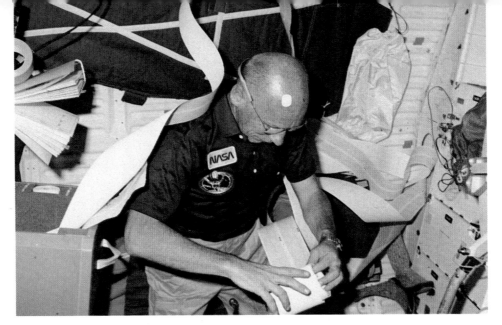

Astronaut William E. Thornton (above) ran biomedical experiments while the Challenger space shuttle orbited the earth. Astronaut Thomas K. Mattingly II (below) floats in the mid-deck area of the Columbia space shuttle. The suction cups on his shoes could hold him in place if he wanted to stay still.

WHAT IS SPACE LIKE?

What is it like to fly off into space? How does it feel? What do you do up there?

There is no gravity in space. That means that nothing weighs anything. Unless it is tied down, it just floats around.

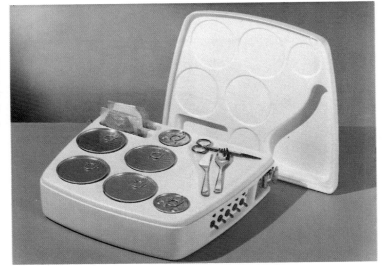

Food tray used on Skylab. Liquids are carried in pouches.

Astronauts have to eat special food in special ways in space. Sometimes the food comes in tubes or plastic bags. A tube of beef, a tube of spinach, a tube of peaches—that's dinner!

John Young didn't like space food very much. So

The crew of the space shuttle *Columbia*. Front row, left to right, Owen K. Garriott, mission specialist, Brewster H. Shaw, Jr., pilot, John W. Young, commander, Robert A.R. Parker, mission specialist. Byron K. Litchtenberg of the Massachusettes Institute of Technology (left) and Ulf Merbold of the Republic of West Germany and the European Space Agency stand in the second row. The *Columbia* flew on November 28, 1983.

he hid a corned beef sandwich in his space suit!

Drinking can also be a problem in space. If an astronaut isn't careful, the liquid will just float away. So astronauts drink out of special containers.

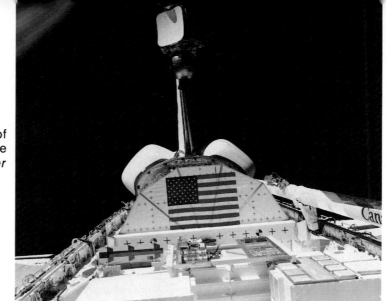

Cargo bay of
the space
shuttle *Challenger*

But astronauts spend most of their time working. They must fly their spacecraft and do special tasks with it. They must be ready to solve mechanical problems—fast. They must do experiments and collect information.

Astronauts Conrad (background) and Kerwin (foreground) worked outside their spacecraft to fix the damaged solar panels on the Skylab space station.

It's a hard job and a dangerous one. But astronauts don't complain. They love their work and they love being in space.

Johnson Space Center in Houston, Texas.

THE RIGHT STUFF

Astronauts work for the National Aeronautics and Space Administration (NASA) near Houston, Texas. Some are members of the armed forces. Some are civilians. Some are

Astronaut Richard M. Truly, center, is the crew commander of the *Challenger* space shuttle. Daniel C. Brandenstein, left, is pilot. The mission specialists are Dale A. Gardner, William E. Thornton, and Guion S. Bluford.

pilots. Some are scientists.

To be an astronaut, you have to have "the right stuff." You must be strong and healthy. Space travel can be hard on the body. Your sight, hearing, and blood pressure must be good.

Dr. Kathryn D. Sullivan (above) climbs into a jet. She is qualified for space shuttle duty. Dr. Sally ride (below) was the first American woman to go into space.

To be an astronaut, you must also know certain things. Pilot astronauts must have flown airplanes a lot. Scientists must have a college degree in engineering, medicine, math, or science.

Astronauts must be brave. Space travel is not always safe. Roger Chaffee, Gus Grissom, and Edward White died in a fire on a launching pad. Several cosmonauts have been killed, too.

Parasail training (left) and on-the-ground training in simulators are part of the astronaut program.

Above all, astronauts must be curious. They must really want to find out what's going on. They must like to ask questions and hunt for the answers. They must not run away from problems.

New astronauts go through a training program.

Astronauts must be in good physical condition. For work outside the spacecraft they must wear pressurized space suits (center).

They learn about space and science. They learn how to move and work without gravity. They learn how to take care of themselves in times of danger. Scientist astronauts must also learn how to fly.

Then the astronauts are trained for their special mission. They learn to use and repair equipment. They learn to work special experiments.

Astronauts spend a lot of time in classrooms. But

Astronauts Bluford (right) and Brand (below) are qualified to fly on space shuttle missions.

they also learn with simulators and airplanes. Sometimes they visit factories and laboratories.

When their training is done, the astronauts start work for NASA. They begin on the ground. They plan missions, invent equipment, and solve problems.

But they all wait and hope that someday they'll be one of the lucky ones who head out into space.

DIFFERENT KINDS OF PEOPLE

Not all astronauts are alike. They come from all over the United States. They have different kinds of families.

Many of the pilot astronauts are military officers. But some aren't. Many have degrees in aeronautical engineering. But some don't.

Most of the astronauts like sports. Ed Aldrin jogs

Geologist Aaron Waters, points out land formations to Roger B. Chaffee (left) who died in 1967 and Russell L. Schweickart (right).

and goes scuba diving. Frank Gordon water skis and sails. Gordon Cooper likes to race cars.

Sally Ride even wanted to be a pro football player when she was twelve years old. But she decided she liked tennis—and space—better.

Some of the astronauts have other hobbies, too. Neil Armstrong and Michael Collins enjoy music. Alan Bean reads and paints. Roger Chaffee liked woodcrafts.

After they've finished space travel, the astronauts do many different things. Some continue to work at NASA. Some go into business. Some become teachers. Some go into politics. Some even write books.

Saturn rocket
carrying Skylab 4
lifts off the
launch pad.

WHAT NEXT?

Astronauts have learned
a lot about space in just a
few years. Space is not
quite so mysterious

anymore. Space travel is not quite so hard.

But what lies ahead? Maybe an orbiting space station. Skylab was a beginning. But a new station could do even more.

It could repair satellites. It could hold scientific experiments. It might even have room for factories to make special drugs to cure diseases like diabetes. It could be a

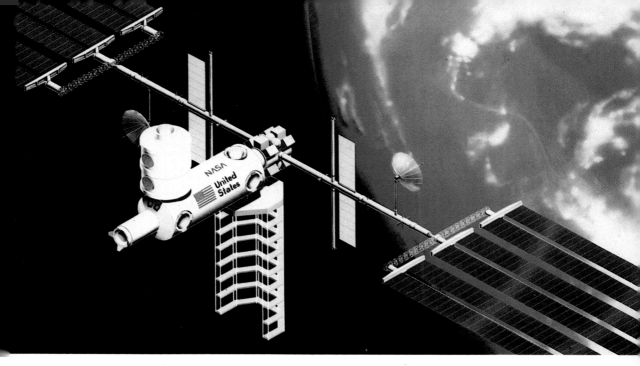

Future space stations will have a utility section, a command and living module, a storage area, a laboratory and a docking facility. Each section will be carried into space by the space shuttle.

spaceport for launching other craft.

And after that? It just might be time for astronauts to build another space station—on the moon.

WORDS YOU SHOULD KNOW

aeronautical(air • oh • NAW • tick • il) — the science and art of
flight
astrophysicist(ast • roh • FIZ • ah • sist) — a scientist who studies
the natural laws of heavenly bodies
capsule(KAP • sil) — a place on a spacecraft for the crew
curious(KYOOR • ee • us) — eager to learn or know
diabetes(dye • ah • BEE • teez) — a physical condition that cannot,
as yet, be cured. People with diabetes take a medicine,
called insulin and/or watch the kinds of food they eat in
order not be dangerously sick.
gravity(GRAV • ih • tee) — the force by which the earth or other
heavenly bodies pull smaller objects toward their centers
launch(LAWNCH) — to send off
mechanical(meh • KAN • ih • kil) — to use machines or tools
mission(MISH • un) — a spacecraft flight with a definite task to
perform
module(MAH • dyool) — separate part of a spacecraft
orbit(OR • bit) — the path a spacecraft takes around the earth
plaque(PLAK) — a metal tablet usually with writing on it.
professional(pro • FESH • un • il) — to make money for work done
simulator(SIM • yoo • lay • ter) — a device in which you can
practice certain skills
task(TASK) — a job

INDEX

About the Author

Carol Greene has written over 30 books for children, plus stories, poems, songs, and filmstrips. She has also worked as a children's editor and a teacher of writing for children. She received a B.A. in English Literature from Park College, Parkville, Missouri, and an M.A. in Musicology from Indiana University. Ms. Greene lives in St. Louis, Missouri. When she isn't writing, she likes to read, travel, sing, do volunteer work at her church—and write some more. Her The Super Snoops and the Missing Sleepers *and* Sandra Day O'Connor, First Woman on the Supreme Court *have also been published by Childrens Press. In the True book series Carol has written about holidays, music, language, and robots.*